Ferndown Library
Tel: 01202 874542

EJANE

GW00870746

- Please return items before closing time on the last date stamped to avoid charges.
- Renew books by phoning 01305 224311 or online www.dorsetforyou.com/libraries
- Items may be returned to any Dorset library.
- Please note that children's books issued on an adult card will incur overdue charges.

Dorset County Council
Library Service

DL/2372 dd05450

CAPTAIN WEIRD

and other curious characters

CAPTAIN WEIRD

and other curious characters

poetry of sorts

selected work written
between 1990 and 2009

. Lloyd

Matador
5 Weir Road
Kibworth Beauchamp
Leicester LE8 0LQ, UK
Tel: (+44) 116 279 2299
Fax: (+44) 116 279 2277
Email: books@troubador.co.uk
Web: www.troubador.co.uk/matador

ISBN 978-1848763-128

Illustrations by the author

British Library Cataloguing in Publication Data.
A catalogue record for this book is available from the British Library.

Typeset in 11pt Palatino by Troubador Publishing Ltd, Leicester, UK

Matador is an imprint of Troubador Publishing Ltd

This book is dedicated
with love
to my daughters
KIRSTY and JOHANNA
the two brightest stars
in the firmament of my life.

And
in memory of my son
CONRAD JAMES ERIC

... people are exasperated by poetry which they do not understand, and contemptuous of poetry which they understand without effort...

T. S. Eliot

Contents

Illustrations

1990-1999

1

Exhibit 'A': the Goliath Stone

Goliath, such a gentle soul,
bemused, perplexed, and a little afraid
to find himself ahead of such
a great and marching army.

His size belied his mental extent,
why an infant would him outdo
on any mental task of note.

Goliath, now dead and gone,
mascot of the Philistines,
had dropped his shield and tried to catch
this stone the baseborn David threw.

* * *

2

Dead On Wednesday

I dreamt I was dead on Wednesday
and awoke to find it not true.
I dreamt I was dead and in your bed.
Dead, but at least next to you.

* * *

3

The Survivor

there must have been about eight of us
all taking up different positions on the platform
I assumed that they were waiting to catch the train
but as the train pulled into the station
we all jumped

* * *

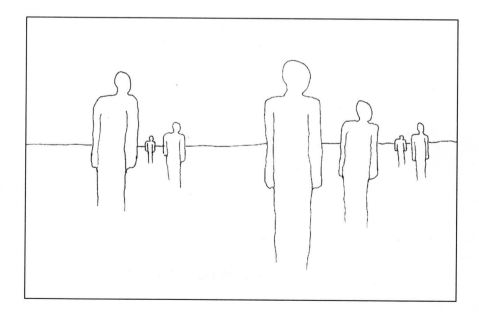

4

The Lovers

We dream,
we dream he and I.
Somme talk,
Verdun listens.

* * *

5

Nails Into Wood

sawing and chiselling and hammering home
nails into wood

planing and gouging and hammering home
nails into wood

gluing and screwing and hammering home
nails into wood

scraping and sanding and hammering home
nails into wood

erecting and fixing and hammering home
nails into wood

knotting and priming and hammering home
nails into wood
nails into wood

* * *

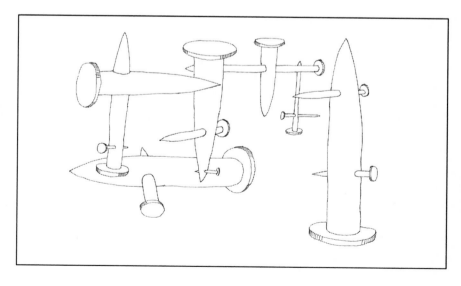

6

once upon a time a traveller returned
from a far off land to find his home
that far off land to which he returned

* * *

7

a homosexual walked past my cubicle today
the door was slightly ajar and I saw him looking in
of course he looked away
when he realised he had been seen
(walked straight by)

sitting naked on the seat inside my cubicle
drying myself after a very satisfying swim
and this homosexual just walks past and peeks in
(I knew he was a homosexual because of his semi-erect penis
and the way his foreskin was pulled back behind his glans)
knew I was not mistaken - that he was a homosexual

I looked out of the cubicle and there he was
the homosexual was looking back at me
looking back at me looking at him and I thought
(not straight away you understand because
I quickly pulled back into my cubicle)
does the homosexual think that I am a homosexual
because I peeped out to see (as if in recognition
of one homosexual acknowledging another)
is that what he thinks?

* * *

8

it's always the dog
that barks in the failing light
that chases the blond youth on his racing bike
into the path of oncoming traffic:
always the dog

it's always the dog
sitting in the cellar with a grin
or sitting in the old man's chair
defying him with a quiet growl and a turned lip:
always the dog

always the dog
yes it's always the dog
with its muzzle tight
against the face of a baby girl
waiting with hungry eyes:
it's always the dog

* * *

9

I walk around your room and dance
walk around your domain and touch
things that you have touched and held

the memory of you they carry
within their structure
within their subatomic particles

electon muon tau
quark and lepton

z and w particles (though short lived)
remember

even the elusive higgs
(it may be there it may be not)
talks to me and tells me
things you will not say
or dare not

touch my hair
            my face
            my lips
with fingers that convey
the memory of your hands
      your face
      your lips

my eyes close and
remembering i am in company

open my eyes and smile
make my excuses and leave

* * *

10

if ee cummings were God, i swear
I'd be on my knees and knightly pray

my eyes fast shut my
hands tight clasped

and off to church, such sweet delight
sing hymns and mumbled amen response

and you why you (with modified anatomy)
his only begotten son would be

* * *

11

if I could which and why and hum
I would reconstitute this cast
and in the out and walk away
would be so far and not the truth
(now to have is i to hide)
your face to carry is to breathe;
to kiss the last kiss of because

* * *

12

too clever by half
this multi-lingual
multi-skilled
multi-bigoted
    bastard

intelligent no doubt
but to use it in this way
to demolish the vulnerable
if not a crime
    close to it

* * *

13

I called to trace my name in the sand;
a feathered memory, wanting
to be more successful than Canute and
hold back this turning tide

> he thought about her all day he thought
> about the impossibility of truth

> what chance has this broken vessel
> (can we tell him?)

> would he comprehend the enormity
> of a concealed answer to an imagined question
> a mere bystander might pose?

> what chance has this broken vessel
> in retaining the substance of faith

I must dance a while, and
pirouette to some conclusion

* * *

14

The Variable Geometry Of The Beach

of course it could be a fairy tale
and have a happy ending
weighing in heavily sighing
like the wind across the strand

occasionally glancing here and there
knowing there is no fairytale ending
the best known is not concealed
and the ending not always happy

to dance beneath the white dome of my skull
as the tide of blood within my brain
washes up on the shore of memory
a shell for you to gather

* * *

15

The Prize

the prize you have won has no value
the goods are shoddy and soiled
you may not or your may
want to give them away
you may think the texture is spoiled

oh, it talks and it laughs and it passes
what passes for water and more
it writes with a pen now and again
but i cannot really tell what it's for

oh yes, it will mimic affection
and tell you things you may want to hear
but why not play safe
just treat it as waste
that way you have nothing to fear

* * *

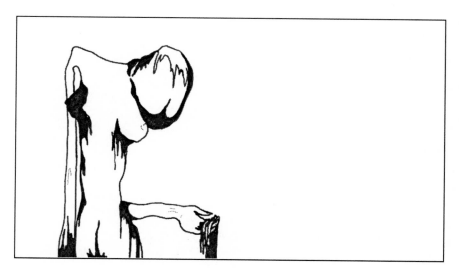

16

the afternoon was heavy in thought
she raised a smile but it was not enough
she shed a tear (but it was not enough)

the afternoon like curtains hung
she coughed and put up her hand
but not to her mouth
rather to be excused

the afternoon was not working well
not working well at all
"if she had sneezed," he thought
"I could have blessed her"

yes
if she had sneezed he would have blessed her
then left

(bodily functions are often
the punctuation in a relationship)

* * *

17

She deserves a tome all to herself,
and she will get a tome all to herself.
Carrying forward to pastures new
that which is written in her name.

It matters not that she may never see
the landscape of this soul exposed,
remodelled as it is, in recognition
of her presence in some life.

* * *

18

Finally Understanding The Meaning Of Bob
Dylan's Song Title:
It Takes A Lot To Laugh/It Takes A Train To Cry

I sat down on the train and wept
I could have laughed
but I wept
I sat on the train (all the passengers stared)
as I wept
and wept
and wept

the conductor sat down and wept
after hearing my tale he wept
on the seat next to me
he just sat right down
then he wept
and wept
and wept

on being served in the station saloon
the bartender (and this is the truth!)
just fell to the floor and wept
he had listened intently
to my story
then wept
(how inept!)

my taxi from the station crashed
but the emergency services accept
the driver after listening to my story lost control
because
he wept
and wept
and wept

after the accident quite a crowd gathered
then in the street they wept
having heard of my plight they wept
it is not really funny
but you just have to laugh
I laughed so much
    I wept

* * *

19

So Precariously Balanced

I live on the edge of the bed, so precariously balanced,
I am reminded of the wall dwellers of Ghormenghast,
hanging as I do, a limpet, between floor and mattress.

I live on the edge of madness, so precariously balanced,
I am reminded of the dilemma of Joseph K, suspended
as I am; a wind chime; to make a noise, or be silent.

I live on the edge of reality, so precariously balanced,
I am reminded of Raskilnikov and his predicament, caught
as I am, between a rock and a hard place; to confess or not.

I live on the edge of life, so precariously balanced,
I am reminded of Schrodinger's cat, confined as I am
within a structure, that may open or may not.

I live on the edge of love, so precariously balanced,
I am reminded of my own limitations, but I can only write.
And so I write but in the process am I betrayed or betrayer?

I live on the edge of time, so precariously balanced,
I am reminded of Eliot's Four Quartets, travelling as do
we all, on this journey from past to future; only present.

I live on the edge of absurdity, so precariously balanced,
I am reminded of the work of Magritte and attempt similar
marks. *Ceci n'est pas une pipe. Ceci n'est pas un poeme.*

I live on the edge of faith, so precariously balanced,
I am reminded of Ballard's Atrocity Exhibition. But
should I try to find the switch and turn the light on?

I live on the edge of paralysis, so precariously balanced,
I am reminded of my doctor's medical report. Confirmation
that I can handle only one language at a time.

I live on the edge of an existential metaphor, so precariously balanced,
I am reminded of Finnegan's Wake; of Heaven's Gate;
of the merry-go-round and of children's laughter.

But

I live on the edge of the bed, so precariously balanced.

* * *

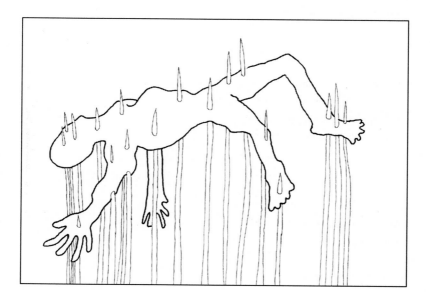

20

i sit here with my dead son forever
and what this gives me
is beyond the written word; the sky
still his canvas

who can understand this
temporal pleasure?

surely not the raggedy man
geeing his horse and cart
and ringing a hand bell
up and down the street

surely not the ice queen
with her fingers of silver
and her limpid stare
that can empty your soul

and

surely not the factory boss
pimping for his second wife
in a desperate attempt to bring
life back to his flaccid member

surely not

surely not the one armed bandit
ringing the changes on the day
and giving out favour
in such a random way

surely not the angle iron
supporting a fence here and there
and making an attempt
at a gate or two

surely not the empty grave
silent and waiting to be fed
with the physical reminder
of some poor bastards life

and

surely not this written word
running here and there
desperately across the page;
geometric insanity

surely not this penultimate verse
with all of its insecurity
so visibly displayed and
so hollow in its laughter

surely not
surely not

* * *

21

Poems

Philip O'Conner writes with intent
to reveal the even tenour of her ways.

i

Included in his son's possessions was the rope he had hung himself with.
"They should not have given me that," he thought, "some of his hair is caught in the
fibre of the rope. No, they should not have given me that."
So he sits and waits for a conclusion, waits in pain: some might say waits in agony.
The conclusion will be different. He does not have his son's courage or despair but
 a full stop at end of the paragraph will be just as final.

ii

Yellow pages unfold with, as yet, an undetermined text. A novel idea, like dust
on a record; an athlete's dilemma.
Light in a yellow-toothed spectrum; on discovering he loves her! Leaves him in fear.
"The route I planned catches her? Maybe." Pose questions like crossword clues.

iii

What inducement this, to fill the first page like sex? Or socks with feet!
Looking, or keeping an eye out for buses and seeing "breast" pluralised,
moving provocatively beneath all manner of exterior garments. Suggestion
of a promised land, the geography of which is described by erect nipples
on varied material.
He understood immediately the relevance of random travel. It has taken
all of his companions a little longer, in some cases they still do not
understand.
One such relates a compound experience they were all supposed to have
shared. It was like hearing a story for the first time; having taken no part
in. Interesting, relevant?
It has been said, "No man is a LiLo". How true.

iv

Simon sits and reflects, facing the window, his reflection
is sitting facing him. Reflecting, it might be said, surely
he has something to offer? Surely he has something
someone wants? He drinks tea in this cafe. "No milk. Thank you".
He appears to be staring at himself. Affect or affected?

v

He arranges himself in a pose more suitable to his needs
and two old ladies sit at the next table

spilling tea and talking shop hoping

the future will be revealed in the spreading
stain on the table cloth

agitated he looks at his watch and counts

now he overhears a child ask "why poppies mummy?"
as donations are made to a distant memory of honour

vi

On leaving he passes a fish vendor plying trade
with frozen and fresh and who can tell the difference
making great gestures with arms and hands
as head and tail are severed

he stops out of ear not out of order
    not that

in the geometry of the house it was true nonetheless
laughter is such a
bitter pill to swallow

vii

the geometry of the house evades and obscure
  angles hide emotive shadows
o yes we know
we all know

not content he pushes her to one side
not to paraphrase
not to quote
not to be
or not

it is an affirmation but one could say he
    was too slow
wracking his brain for long incomprehensible words
to confound the reader but his lack of success drives him
to bite a nail to the quick and then another and then
another

in this half-life he watches from the half-light
as in a warm but dimly lit room she sits
  not quite naked
she touches and there is a parting of flesh an
    opening of soul
the landing in shadow the mirror at her feet
yes she is watched as hands o both
    hands
open her and play
    music
and as the volume rises in her veins she kneels
astride the mirror until its cool surface kisses her
    thigh
the observer observes and she knows as
her eyes close and the music
    is
as her eyes close

the geometry of the house surrounds her

when he has departed she
will walk with that same mirror through this house
recording every geometric shape
every angle therein contained

still kneeling
she pushes her legs so wide so
    wide she touches the mirror
some mythological beast screams at her
    to come

collapse and smile and in that half-life half-light
  the geometry of the house is fractured

later the mirror is replaced
and she smiles and kisses the glass
that holds forever the memory of her
    sex
she refused then and refuses still
to clean the glass

he was still thinking and fell through the open door
desperately needing a coherent hand

numeric clues are so obscure that he can only
    dream of the geometry of the house

* * *

22

Half-Life

half-life n (1907)
1: the time required for half of something to undergo a process:
 as a: the time required for half of the atoms of a radioactive substance to become disintegrated
b: the time required for half the amount of the substance (as a drug, radioactive tracer, or pesticide) in or introduced into a living system or ecosystem to be eliminated or disintegrated by natural processes
2: a period of usefulness of popularity preceding decline of obsolescence - slang usually has a short half-life

PART 1
A prototype replacement for memory:

1   History presented as a perpetual animated cartoon,
    its major players reduced to cardboard cut-outs
    to be blown away at some future execution.
    The veneer of our own past protects; underarm deodorant we use,
    we do not bowl like that.
    Parallel line we draw, but conclusions?

2   Are we therefore destined only to make drafts?
    Our mouths and arms effectively do that!
    Draught after draught.
    To include a numbered appendix, will it add weight
    or lessen the significance of the main body of text?
    Man has been known to be wrong in the past,
    and demonstrably so.

3   Touch the ground with the palm of the hand
    whilst casting an eye to the heavens and
    as memories alight the risks are revealed; taken
    for nought are incoherent decisions.

4   Planning something of importance; architectural.
     Important possibly, but as horrific as this?
     A huge structure emerges. Plans once concealed, now revealed,
     congeal in the head and a draft eventually emerges onto paper.

5   On exiting this edifice he slips and cuts abstract arcs in the ether with his limbs
     as they flail, concluding this exercise on his arse: humiliation on a grand scale.
     Is the blood that caused the fall his own?
     The horror, the horror!

6   Postures adopted, wayward children of the past, cannot be
     relied upon as once they were.
     The subtle 'snap' of breaking bones; a starling's wing
     embracing the cheek of a blind girl; a
     limb distorted over an iron support.

7   This then, the only reliable document
     to give any clue to the truth, to the logic, to
     the very existence of man. How
     many a player participates, periodically performing?

8   The resumption of visionary tactics
     to deceive the audience, which may include you, dear reader,
     a victim of some awful conspiracy.

9   The subject's suited shadow leaves the car
     in disguise. Ah! We know that smile, We know it
     well. We know of the search; profit and loss.

10   Occasionally the weather interferes. This weather, as inconsistent as
     it is irrelevant. One days weather can be equated to more
     than the delay of twenty-four hours. Rain speeds this eternal skid.
     Brakes can stop and bones can break; fragmented dreams of another land.

11   Spare a thought for the shrew when the wind bites and the mercury contracts,
     spare a thought won't you, as he speeds beneath the ice
     in a perpetual search for food. This poor water shrew
     must move, move and eat. Eat, eat through
     the cold and whipped white wild wilderness of winter.

12 Oh yes, we hear the cries, we hear the comments made.
    Look into the faces of lost friends and wonder.
    We laughed before the invention of the drain, before the echo of a sigh,
    before the bridging of teeth. Who exactly is?
    A conflict: this written word versus your thought pattern, dear reader.
    Without a prescient knowledge this must appear to be gibberish.
    But can you not see? Future ceremonies
    hailing a loser on the winner's rostrum!

13 A sore, like the torn-out last page of a novel
    running before the wind across a beach, disfigures this face.
    Red flashing lights are synchronised exactly with a throbbing pain.
    Sand flies crawl on an open wound
    but there is no relief in this distraction. A memory
    from a tropical beach: an open anus pushed into the sand
    taking on a cargo.

14 If we are to understand anything of this we must forget
    how to hate. If we must talk ill of anyone let them at least be dead.
    And acknowledge this can be difficult. As
    the adulterer returns home in the small hours to reflect upon his guilt,
    to terrorise his wife with accusation and abuse;
    as bombs are blessed with prayer; as towns with fire. Ah! You see it!
    The hypocritical head of man exposed.

15 Procrastination, good afternoon! Can we help it?
    Dance on painted fences and sell trinkets at exorbitant prices;
    reward yourself with doubt?

16 Place carefully this rubbish, stack carefully these bags.
    To refer to it, split a bag, the relevant bag, thrust in a hand
    and carefully extract something dank and foul-smelling,
    then excite it for a fluid answer. Most of this will die, maybe all.

17 At the bottom of the page a cross is not always found.
    What are these marks, what do they represent? Faces in conflict.
    Dear reader, can you see it? Time, like dice, like semen, can fall
    with or without favour.

18 An age in Arabian Nights rapidly approaches. Who among the congregation
    will celebrate this coming event? Will drink from his cupped hand
    cooling seed?

19 Think well of this collective. To censor is to be censored,
    to condemn is to be condemned. No escape. Modification,
    a continual process; bones of iron to silicon, feet from flesh and bone
    to tracked appendages. Impossible edifice; man.

20 Flight will come, we have to promise it to ourselves and it will come.
    Something within will burst forth and we will fly. The future therein lies.
    Look back only for salt. The plaque on the wall
    adheres less well than on teeth; blood less well than conscience.

21 At the stops, do it at the stops. Mumbled narrative.
    But who's? No relief.

22 There is always something to be done. Dragging this implement
    on an erratic course across this desert of page
    creating an image the reader fails to understand; the eye is still held.

23 The dog barks, pisses then barks again. The moon watches.
    The dog chases its tail. In spinning turns a light first off, then on,
    and has nothing to do with shadow. Again and again.
    A phrase comes to mind, "It's always the dog, always the dog."

24 There is no such thing as age. Age is myth, a device
    to enable those with more years to be correct.

25 The spider sky tears out our guts.
    The next world comes before us. The wet, the stain, the bloody shit,
    haunt the doctor like a cross. A game is played, triggered
    by this prototype memory. Sickness brings it all back.
    All fall what? Down...

26 Do we address you then? We see your eyes, could name you.

27 Dance you bastard, dance! Listen and laugh to the failing of memory.
    The ragged hymen is all the proof we need to indicate penetration.

28 A fish, a pal, a name, a friend of mine? All of these.
   Look, search in the mince for the answer to this.
   Only hot-headed virgins pass water as truth.

29 We could, we really could set clues for God
   and leave Him puzzled. Alternatively we could not
   set clues and still leave God with egg on His face! Her face?
   Emphatic, are we not? And why not!
   Punctuation equals explanation.

30 We hear of plates. Tectonics move us
   from where to then. And we carry them
   in our mouth and eat off them. Look, we
   just want to be there, we just want to see…

31 Write yourself to sleep, Frank.
   You can handle this, can't you?
   You may scream a little, if provoked.
   Take no notice, it's nothing.

32 How vulnerable is he?
   Daughters' leave a trace in memory.
   He must stop this habit, refusing
   to quote Shakespeare out of season.
   Stop that! Stop, the geometry is too clever.

33 A hymn is written but not sung, if it were
   it would tell of the age at dawn. We are sentenced to death, laughing
   at the numerous entries filling this replacement for memory.

34 An understanding missed; a friend adrift, a love hanging
   like reluctant lightening in the fabric of emotion.

35 He plans. They are driving him into
   the welcoming arms of the asylum.
   Is this a "text book" case?
   Out to lunch is, after all, out to lunch.

36 They thought hard and remembered his words
   "Don't look," and thought on, "a clue, this is a clue."
   To a game of chance, perhaps?

37 Easy to try to be. Isn't it
easier to drink urine from a cup
than from the point of emission?

38 Look, you can laugh and no one will
object, but there is one small favour to ask.
Please tell those assembled where exactly this is?

39 Where were we?

40 A telephone at some distant location rings but remains unanswered.
Sounding as clear as a bell: is the room in which it tolls empty, or
does someone sit and smile at the pain inflicted?

41 The mythology of fact passes by, a page at time.

42 Under this hand a landscape evolves, automatically
the pen traces a vision of apparent wonder.
Who is the originator of this?

43 The sun sets. It could just as easily be rising.

44 Wait! We have some understanding here. Time
is not directional. We make the wrong assumptions.

45 Do you not recognise this country? A song
and the ghost music of the poet, swimming with the tide
past King Charles dock, all bright, all bright and patterned glass.
The light dances, reflected across the river. A song in lights
accompanied by the outgoing tide. Lost cities built with lost skills.
He looks down from his creation to his hands. "Did I build that?"
It is a genuine question he asks, still doubting. He picks up a stone
and throws it into the Thames, misses the expected splash
but is startled by the unexpected cry.

46 "David! David!" No use, it is no use
calling out his name. She dances, blames him
yet dances on and on in time, not of it. Later
she informs him that it was to welcome in the New Year.
He wishes he were that old, to have someone
dance like that. This New Year, this
modern myth with little basis in fact.

47　We move into peripheral vision for answers
　　to these unexpected questions
　　on the nature of entropy.
　　Dogs bark; monkeys climb.

48　Staying awake with great difficulty, staring
　　into the night, forcing his eyes wide open, forcing
　　her legs to part, forcing her to force herself to smile. A lesson
　　from the dark no doubt. Listening skills enhance
　　the well-being of this house as behind the skirting
　　something moves. Within the solid concrete walls something moves.
　　Services concealed carry, as well as the functions they perform, sound.
　　Another clue here. The ratio of noise to sleep, sleep to rain, et cetera.

49　To push the pram, to dance that same old tired dance, why, we must be flawed.
　　If man were to really know. Predictions on the size and the age of the universe
　　are so hopelessly inaccurate. If we were to know then
　　how would we, how could we, cope with such knowledge? Running, always
　　running to catch up. So what! Movement is the thing.
　　Yes that's it! Movement. Keep moving. Walter walks on water, walks
　　across the lake. Dry like ice. He comments to this author,
　　"Notes! Is that all you can do, write notes?!" Laugh, it is all we can do, it is
　　all we can do apart from taking notes. So that's it? No, don't laugh.
　　All great men are flawed. J. Edgar was no great shakes
　　but he was a dab hand at the rouge. The flaw is always hypocrisy.
　　Does this repetition of the obvious weaken or emphasise its impact?
　　Reader, we do not call upon you to judge,
　　just to be patient.

50　Someone speaks, "Don't
　　be entrapped by these words, please." She smiles
　　but does not understand. He writes with such confusion
　　she fears she will never be caught. Dark matter
　　concealed at heart. The universe is made of something we cannot see
　　yet has a physical presence, enabling us to complete a mathematical picture of it.
　　We cut the lugs off jigsaw pieces to make them fit,
　　to complete a version of reality;
　　chaos at the edge of symmetry.

* * *

PART 2

APPENDIX:
confusion after the event

1   mixed media;
    enterprising young men in knee-length raincoats
    waltz like tornados and
    echo with rage

2   friends in a frenzy and
    artichoke soup for which there is
    no answer

3   should it not be chilled?
    has no one the heart to tell them?

4   fear like lice
    an infestation of the head
    water down the throat of a drain
    abroad a monsoon ditch is filled

5   comments fall from a mouth unseen
    kick over atavistic traces
    this in turn turns heads
    making sense and saving face;
    a matter of principle

6   some other philosophy not claimed
    another meal with difficulty
    digested
    "the password
    the password" someone shouts
    turning and closing doors and thinking
    "thank God it is not a matter of life and death"

7   who
    among us finds this
    clever

8   and who knows
      the password?

9   holding out a shaking hand
      to count nails chewed

10 can you guess or
      is this devastation confined to
      the Fibonacci sequence?

11 we are back
      numerically speaking
      (one two three)
      with the waltz
      (one two three)
      (one two three)

12 four five six
      and the remaining digits decline

13 seven even more so
      (eight nine ten)

14 ten times two
      is no more than the sum total of
      fingers and toes

15 barrow boys shout all day
      and make amends
      by tempting middle-aged menopausal women
      into disclosures they would not have otherwise made

16 turn your head then
      away from stinking meat and fish

17 pray for rain or
      railings around the park

18 coherence is in embryo here
      not just on inaccessible autopilot
      because that is not it
      not it at all

19 apologies now or later?

20 the autocratic assumption
    that the philosophy herein contained
    has no value
    leaves a vacuum of doubt

21 identity

22 speed and efficiency
    and rattling noises in the attic
    chairs in the cellar
    are a sort of balance
    a trick of the heart

23 (a mother of a question
    to ask of the daughter)

24 fillet of plaice
    and table settings
    displaying death
    disguised as art

25 the chef
    the chef

26 the audience applaud
    but some stay silent
    and do not rise for the guilt they share
    (a pastime we have taken pleasure in)

27 great men of science and philosophers
    intellectuals all
    tell us there is no choice
    no choice at all

28 must we believe them?
    do they talk to themselves?

29 such arguments have no logic

30 what time is this?
    now is the who and the how
    and noise is as the baby cries
    in the night possibly more trouble for us all

31 hand goes to sleep-filled eye
    to pick out solid matter therein congealed
    restoring sight to the temporarily blind
    and nature courses like the hare
    through the ravaged body
    and veins like spaghetti hang
    suspended in this body politic
    erected upon a frame of chalk
    unable to support itself unaided

32 haunted by a name from pages
    blank; unwritten stories

33 description of a future event
    unimagined and undreamt of as yet

34 a cross-reference;
    an angry silence
    will not lessen this

35 the allocation of guilt has
    been made allegedly

36 is it too easy then to fill
    these lines
    this rhetoric?

37 seeing the hint of disbelief
    an explanation is required

38 the flame in the fire
    holds the answer

39 ask where it is and
    be given a light

40 where is the age that has less to do with age
    and what is the age on asking?

41 catch up with the light and
    link arms with a drowning man

42 by the afternoon all will seem
    normal

43 after a false dawn to accompany
    this false prophet

44 stories told to children
    foretell of this and
    of other events

45 of other events to come to pass like
    a shadow on the sea
    vague and ill-defined

46 (a catching up process
    mouse with cat -
    something like that)

47 but then violence is never an answer
    never a prayer for the blind
    (a discourse for the wealthy perhaps)

48 are we then
    never to expect an answer?

49 they have a choice now of which funeral to attend -
   that of the hanged man
   or that of their friend

50 "it's over
   can we take him down now?
   can we please
   take
   him
   down?"

* * *

23

i know it's daft
i know it's absurd
but i've just thought of a poem
with only one word

* * *

24

trying to work it out she finds it extremely difficult
to rationalise the intricacy and vagueness of this particular relationship
giving up she points the remote control at the TV
and watches yet another repeat of an endless progression
of excursions 'boldly going...'

"why" she muses "they only had to take one little trip to my crotch"
then thinks about her selection of the word chosen
to describe her virgin sex
and laughs uncomfortably to herself
her cat wakes and eyes his mistress and wonders
in a typically cat type way
what exactly is going on inside her head
does she know herself, as the hapless cat is evicted from her lap
she walks out of the living room and heads for the bathroom
leaving Captain Kirk and crew to their fate

on hearing water gushing into the bath the creature
executes a hasty retreat via the cat flap into the garden

soon safely concealed up a tree muses
"I've seen this movie before"

  * * *

25

1/10

3   many a road travelled here i have and felt
the inside of many a white thigh
observed also anatomical parts of an omnibus

5   many lanes walked and stalled
stabled horses neighboured laughter
mechanical shovel snaps up
undemocratic motions passed
from high places (not like snow)

2   many breaths inhaled are we and you
without we would not be or do

4   many is not all; a button not yet depressed
i wanted cummings as a friend and ee
became a love in soft red word
his ghost (assumption here) reads this wrote

6   many paved and elevated
trodden horse shit underfoot
rabbit gutter meanderings
excuse machine works overtime
faith only is religion if we are;
seek a symbol to hang a hat on

7   many fast slow stop dead still
flatland is a demographic feature
wasteland a state of mind
one mans rubbish another's gold
contemplating short line parallel tracks
steam from engines past
sunflower oil across an appreciative face

8   many times i have often prayed
    the world breaks down on a bank holiday monday
    there are even bodily functions we have to queue for
    jack the lad o he was real uh
    heliotrope canopy concealed children
    flowers of our race spinning a free ride
    adventure playground saturation mindfuck
    we turn with them into donk donkey donkeys

10 many a potion consumed before success
    twisted limb and warped bone
    product of a distorted point of view
    experiments with rats et al
    volunteer and victim both
    the physician drinks becomes Hyde
    and seeks out fair game abroad
    to pollute to choke and spill
    defective seed against
    another cheek turned

9   many a flower in the dust
    ideas fall on a pad
    like doodles or lotteries drawn
    a game of chance to play
    or is it better as a participant;
    apple trees to climb and fall
    from Grace
    and squash bugs underfoot
    in staccato midnight blooming

1   many a last line to an inconclusive poem

* * *

26

at some personal risk and at great length
(to wave a wand is not nearly enough)
at some personal risk and at a great distance
to wave a hand in a storm
                              reckless in the extreme

falling hands and dogs upon the deck
fail to impress the crowd assembled
with its dogs and its falling hands
"man overboard!" a sailor shouts
                              but who listens?

not the dogs no not the dogs and
surely not the falling falling hands
or the blind girl at the baby grand
playing out the passing of the day
                              not drowning but waving

* * *

27

Captain Weird

i

Captain Weird parks the car
lowers his head and walks away
goes into his house and sits
down at the kitchen table

a knock at the door tells him
it is time to argue with the neighbours
he gets up from the table and
dons his cap and cape

ageing slightly he opens the door
a cackle of voices assail his ears
(the Captain
being partially deaf
has the upper hand)

with a wave and a look
he has their complete attention
with a shout and a gesture
they disappear into the ground

ii

I have fallen in love with
a girl in my dreams
I did not actually see her
but her presence was tangible
in my dreams

down endless corridors
I followed her
up and down stairs
through a dark dank cellar
room after empty room
but never quite catching
a glimpse of her;
on finding her bedroom
lay in wait

iii

Captain Weird rides roughshod
over any dreams of substance
his wife might have;
the laughter and the noise
have gone from his life

he raises his hoe heavenward
shaking it in defiance
at his waning faculties
"Cinderella will go to the ball" he remarks

"… all they ever do
is read" his wife says
of the neighbours
their shit-stained sheets
she washes weekly
as if trying to remove
some remnant from their dreams
mesmerised she watches
soiled water disappear

iv

daughters are a blessing and
if there is nothing else
to justify this life
then let it be daughters

words like "love"
do not enough do
not convey

and do they ever consider
their dead brother
his image a faded
black and white photograph

and do they ever consider
Captain Weird and his regalia;
demented gardener
out of tune
out of step and
time

v

Captain Weird and his animal family
now camped on the village green
pumping up water from a standpipe
then pissing and defecating
from the kerbs edge

"they wont be there long"
a passer-by comments
"I am not so sure" another remarks
"I have heard it said
the Captains lost"
"he is
he is that"

vi

vee one (or six in roman numerals)
indicate alternative trajectories
and we
astride this beast of time
blindly gallop
along one or the other

* * *

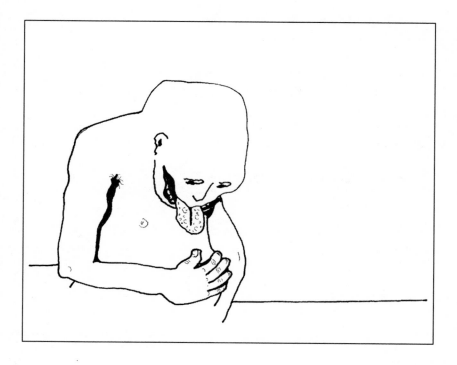

28

The Ambidextrous Smoker

From time to time; we open with
the inevitable intrusion of chance.

From hand to hand; a cigarette moves
as if by magic thus transferred.

From mouth to mouth; a sentence passed,
sentiment not exactly expressed.

From kiss to kiss; tentative, immobilised,
stolen time solidified.

From limb to limb; visions of a future
tense. Here, entangled memory forgets.

From heart to heart; misunderstood as
in the desert words fall like rain.

From cheek to cheek; to pirouette on the ceiling
in defiance of gravity.

From eye to eye; reflections of desire
and cruelty, unseen.

From tongue to tongue; spitting back the spoken word
like saliva.

From finger to finger; prodding, pointing
stabbing the air with accusation.

From thumb to thumb; around which neck?
Throttled, strangled, severed, torn.

From face to face; back to back,
secret words of bitterness.

From grimace to grimace; pulling faces;
carcasses in the coloured rain.

From angle to angle; projected dream.
Erotic bliss or nightmare eye?

From train to train; vehicle or thought?
A child's dream, partially realised.

From friend to friend; a factor not considered
here, passing too quickly.

From dust to dust; names concealed, but
the wind of time may reveal them.

From beach to beach; a tired vessel watched,
a figure stands on the foreshore; waves.

From truth to truth; concealed facts, once guessed at
eventually revealed, offer no consolation

From strength to strength; alone
in shadow, something disturbs.

From birth to birth; increased options,
not always available to the crowd.

From day to day; interspersed by a darkness:
call it night.

From season to season; perambulation through time,
metamorphosis for the soul.

From photograph to photograph; awkward
instant images of time.

From car to car; these
invisible occupants of the car egg.

From scream to scream; listen to the
foreclosing silence; footfall after searching footfall.

From death to death; spinning forever,
to this inevitable conclusion

From time to time; remember this
the ambidextrous smoker; I.

* * *

29

This Is The Law

this is the law
of diminishing returns
this is the law

this is the call
the wilderness philosopher makes
as the light dies

this is the feast
set before all men
on the night of the hanging

this is the sound
women in Africa hear
in their sleep

this is the train
that carries forlorn hope
to the dying

this is a word
next to another word
next to another

this is the seed
falling from spend loins
into an empty place

this is the pain
suffered by martyrs
if that is their choice

this is the rhetoric
issuing forth from
the politicians arse

this is the species
forever on
the brink of extinction

this is the deviant action
of daughters dancing
into the west wind

this is the sky
and this is the See
haunting our lives

this is the celebrity
as seen on the silver screen
but not with a smile

this is the day
holding our memories
dear to our ancestral heart

this is the wisdom
the wisdom of Solomon
so they tell me

and this is
the continuing saga of this is
this is

* * *

30

no one writes letters to Arnold
and no one writes to me
but it could get better
I could write a letter
to myself

and to Arnold?
maybe...

* * *

31

a voice i am familiar with, the name less so, calls
and makes a solemn proclamation; i do not
want to hear this, do not want to erase
an impossible image of cock and cunt dancing
forward, re-writing history, slowing time
                                        to a standstill

a voice i am familiar with, whispered halo; a
fly circumnavigates my head, speaks and
makes a solemn proclamation, referring obliquely
to stony ground, stony, stony barren ground, not
quite the once envisaged dance of cock and cunt coming
                                        to a standstill

a voice i am familiar with silences the night, screaming
for a halt to this apparent assault upon her soul
but i am only guilty of an extravagant transparency
look away then from intelligent design, as cock and cunt
lock in that awful embrace and eventually move
                                        to a standstill

* * *

32

The Hare Is A Beast

the hare is a beast that is hunted
and kippers are fish, but not fried
a wart 'neath the foreskin discovered
after its owner has died

young Molly sits on a bucket
this has little or no meaning for me
but a kipper once concealed
is now gloriously revealed
(I think I'll have two for my tea)

a cow is a beast meant for milking
or killing and cooking and that
but my poetry masquerades and evades;
can you make any sense out of hats?

why, I know they are for the wearing
on a head (maybe yours) I believe
on being beaten at chess
must ask for a rest
achiever's achievement achieved

* * *

33

Coherence

Coherence
an Indian friend with a laugh of a young girl
kissed the wind on naked feet
his flame black eyes lit the night
his smile brought me close to tears

Coherence
through the time of his earthly existence
wrote not one single word
spoke seldom
yet left an indelible mark on the face of time

my friend
a memory of him standing in the rain
his wet body reminiscent of
the wind-swept beach we played on
as children with impossible dreams

my friend
still now but never still
with me until we meet again
wings carry him
through the labyrinth of my soul

* * *

34

Retrospective

difficult but not impossible
blocked but not impassable
animated but not imbued
with any idea but this

the forehead is marked but identification
still difficult
but not impossible

the bowels are blocked but
given an enema or two
not impassable

the animation technique used
leaves the Harlequin dancing

* * *

35

In Anticipation Of Grief
or the architecture of hell

memory is not the path to the past
we perceive it to be

the precedent memory sets
though flawed, is believed

loss of memory, the anaesthetic

persistence of memory, the pain

* * *

36

Vague

vague
more vague
most vague

offended
more offended
most offended

dream
more dreamt of
most dreamt of

laughs
more
most

quick
more haste
less speed

* * *

37

throw the ball
catch the ball
throw the ball
run

throw the ball
drop the ball
kick the ball
run

after the ball
            is over

* * *

38

i want to be famous for someone
so can i be famous for you?
can i be famous, o please say yes
say i can be famous for you

i will need a little encouragement
a push now and again it is true
but then i'll be famous, really famous
and all because of you

i know, i know it's not easy
not such a simple thing to do
to become famous, so famously famous
but i would, i would do it for you

* * *

2000-2009

39

a subtle movement of the lips
produces no audible sound: he cannot read
a meaning in their abstract geometry

he looks and wonders, 'what are they
whispering?' (if indeed any method
of communication is employed)
they cross the room, passing by so close,
so close - why he could just reach out and
touch, and embrace their secret language
to press his lips against them, to prise apart
with his tongue these silent sirens,
then cautiously explore their interior architecture;

         mouth to mouth

* * *

40

every original version is
a construct of its own time

it is difficult to imagine
not being here

to fully comprehend
things fall apart

on departure all
questions are answered

and the corollary
is nothing matters

a journey begins;
a destination reached

* * *

41

mischief makes for idle minds as elephants to trees;
a metaphor for the terminally deluded
are we to witness here a definitive
version of the 21st century zeitgeist?

and to avoid the question
remove the plural and reverse the first line

* * *

42

FLUX

compositions conceived as floating elements, functioning like dreams
condensed then displayed, disembodied, torn away from the flesh of the
world
the appearance of an edge as being definitive is false; the border between this
and after
to achieve an apparent realisation without ambiguity or contradiction; this
absolute rigidity of appearance seemingly reducing the possibility of variation
is false

       all is in flux
       and at the edge
       more so

* * *

43

The Only One

this 'first of many' is up and too
strong (unlike the wind) and Wilde,
his attic portrait on his head.
Poe-faced and tap tap tapping,
asking to be let back in
right to the neverwhere of left,
breaking rocks and hearts: his own
the 'first of many,' the only one

* * *

44

the past and future fragments herein contained
make the whole more substantial than it at first appears
Ann Margaret[1] with scissors, snip, snip, snipping, made
unrelated patterns appear to fit together
within the parameter of a twentieth-century paradigm

* * *

1 In the film 'The Cincinnati Kid' with Steve McQueen in the title role.

45

Transparent

transparent *adj.*
1. permitting the uninterrupted passage of light; clear.
2. easy to see through, understand, or recognise; obvious.
3. candid, open or frank.

PART ONE: **trajectory over Europe**
              an indicator; line

Having a path to follow, an indication of the direction of travel.
A discontinued line of poetry; memory traversing dawn.

This voyage we are committed to. No turning back, no
astonishment at the havoc left in our wake.
'Lookout!!' a yell, a warning travelling at the speed of sound
still cannot prevent the apple's fall.

Free will, free wheel,
downhill, down hill, down down hill;
bus stop at the bottom indicates halt.

       Nine lines to fill,
       nine lives have cats,
       in our nine lives this
       beast of burden.

Shaded eye,
hooded sleep;
deaf owl.

Fruit left on the table is a talking point for some.
Now eating from a can, freshly displayed and
thrown up as a question mark.

A surname
or well known phrase -

carnival carnivores, cantankerous creatures
cart-wheeling, cavorting; carefully constructed
conundrums can quickly compound the case in question -
could any of the crowd be in collusion here?

Talking, taking that long, too,
naked only dancers will not talk;
remembered kisses, silent words.

(over our heads, mostly
missile crisis)

PART TWO: **drug abuse in africa**
             doppelganger

i   i

amorphous desire shapes this dream   hollow words shadow people give
hollow words shadow people give   no shelter from abusive guests

no shelter from abusive guests   no respite for an isolated mind
no respite for an isolated mind   a productive combination of the two

a productive combination of the two not necessarily productive thought
not necessarily productive thought   rainy days in obscure places

rainy days in obscure places   taxi across the face of africa in pursuit
taxi across the face of africa in pursuit   untranslatable languages from our past

untranslatable languages from our past   a relief from staccato death in the afternoon
a relief from staccato death in the afternoon   amorphous desire shapes this dream

ii   ii

repetitive images give an indication   an obsession; paranoia of limitation
an obsession; paranoia of limitation   in this field of vision

in this field of vision   in the vocabulary of time
in the vocabulary of time   great beasts of burden

great beasts of burden   animals of lust
animals of lust   poets and seminal painters

poets and seminal painters   chiselling away at the metaphysical
chiselling away at the metaphysical   in pursuit of impossible constructs

in pursuit of impossible constructs   creation of an alternate God
creation of an alternate God   repetitive images give an indication

77

iii

the Nile - a river in africa perhaps
the whispered name of a friend

in the dark a homage paid to an ancient king
show respect and we fall to our knees

illusory gains wasted on the vernacular
intravenous administration of addictive drugs

being both a social and physical shock
depending on the dosage

then Latin or French insertions here
how much culture can be borne

iv

time makes great historians of us all
great poets too will be made aware

grand and multi-coloured vision
no sight given to the clouded eye

no speech to the silent tongue
no meaning to well-spoken words

the occasional sound in a deaf ear
no guarantee that the truth will be heard

to taste again does not make bitter sweet
just this then nothing – touch

iii

the whispered name of a friend
in the dark a homage paid to an ancient king

show respect and we fall to our knees
illusory gains wasted on the vernacular

intravenous administration of addictive drugs
being both a social and physical shock

depending on the dosage
then Latin or French insertions here

how much culture can be borne
the Nile - a river in africa perhaps

iv

great poets too will be made aware
grand and multi-coloured vision

no sight given to the clouded eye
no speech to the silent tongue

no meaning to well-spoken words
the occasional sound in a deaf ear

no guarantee that the truth will be heard
to taste again does not make bitter sweet

just this then nothing - touch
time makes great historians of us all

PART THREE: **antipodean haemorrhage**
a desert smile across wasted plates
wine stains on linen
cutlery in disarray;
meal raped

Luxury Liner earth takes us on this cosmic cruise, on automatic pilot and faith;
no Captain visible at the helm. We have the choice of class; which
way to travel, depending on decisions made, or not. We all eat
from the place of our choosing but still obscured is the Captain's table.
Who is sitting there?

High flying birds take a southern path on instinct, on hope. Trusting
that the land they seek
will enter their vision, will be
a just reward for their effort.
Eventually.

A crowded Underground disturbs
this minor train of thought; a broken pickaxe handle makes
the excavation of mineral wealth difficult in the extreme.

The concealed library of the Native American
no living soul has seen. Predictions about
the destiny of Man are interrupted by a knock.
'Is that you?'

Ancient men, tales between their legs oft told,
see decay in sex: a luxury high.
Apertures of old remembered.

PART FOUR: **arctic heart**
               uncontrolled, the mouth moves
               as the mind moves mountains

i   Read this on the basis of some logic contained herein,

ii   annotate nightmares and erotic dreams with past and future tense.

iii   Water if congealed like blood, would make the consumption of it more
      difficult, but not impossible.

iv   Roman numerals echo significant architecture apparently,

v   poetry in crowded bars; distraction at each compass point.

vi   Gas as a vehicle for suicide can give too many variables.

vii   Here is, of course, a resonant frequency for an earring in a pierced ear. Deaf?

viii The deterioration of this arctic heart; a cold room in a vessel adrift.

ix   It is becoming apparent that conclusions are being drawn here;

x   the first parachute jump was a revelation; information theory
      gave no indication of a soft landing.

xi   Given the correct circumstance, the appropriate globe to circumnavigate
      apparently; age in time is equal to distance.

xii   Mirror! Mirror, who dares to question, to reinforce known answers?

xiii Truth is evasive, and this too is not always an accurate reflection on water.

xiv   Blood on the sheets; no crime here,

xv   wind in the eye, no tear.

xvi   Billowed fabric of dream, landscaped,

xvii   recurring images of the night-watchman's tin cup; tattoo,

xviii   reflecting upon an age, not believing it will be reached.

xix   Black Dog is an abusive salt, he does not take kindly to
         verbosity.

xx   Melting to the point of new or freezing to the bone.

xxi   Panic in the air! Is this live or not?

xxii   Incinerated behind the bicycle shed; adults in training.

xxiii   Flushed with what, success or fear?

xxiv   Water to wash away a foul taste from the mouth leaves no stain.

xxv   Nailed to the cross, in memory of a loved one

xxvi   abandoned, this God plots His revenge.

xxvii   Secret lives chronicled in contemporary music; listen, no piano here.

xxviii   Lightening strikes the eye of the cuckold.

xxix   Crouching, frightened, hiding behind the accident debris, calling, 'Father?'

xxx   He remembers having slept here once. Race memory;

xxxi   strength in the knowledge of this quiet love,

xxxii   having now been to where there was once only dream.

PART FIVE   **rhododendron waltz**
              laughter, madness, epilepsy, exercise
              sex; everything fits

The music began and it was almost too easy to find a partner.
In the open air under a velarium punctuated with stars, whirling
through this geometric garden; a mystery concealed by angles.
A most natural act in an unnatural environment. The emphasis here
is too strong, perhaps.

This awesome design may indicate a form of control
we seek to acknowledge but dare not name.
A voice may be heard, 'to whom does this garden belong?' but
an answer is seldom sought, let alone expected.

There is no more perfection
in the harmony and balance of the universe than here.
With the possibility of the infinity of alternatives it appears
only duplication is sought.

* * *

46

Chimes At Midnight

i

the first the last and the lazy
collect this assemblage of 'cool'
their definition of a definitive role
for Welles in the part as the fool
the return of rhythm is manifest
equivalent of wearing one's pride
stapled securely to one's chest
not quite concealing the bride

ii

a second in time quite hazy
obscured by clouds as a rule
meaning or meanings not definite
or prescriptive yet still a literary tool
apparently concealed in shadow
not first not second but next
touched by the Devils mantle
ensure even the worthy are vexed

iii

and a third mentioned in passing
is all too apparently false
just relax for a while in the bathtub
ask the oriental lady for a waltz
as in a monochrome landscape
the Moor and the Dane try hard
adopt their positions and perpetually repeat
an apothegm penned by the Bard

* * *

47

Three Kings

GOLDIE   it is a very tall order indeed
to attempt an ascent and succeed
then remain unknown
and not answer the phone
as the media demand that you bleed

FRANKLY   it is a very tall story so how
did we ever believe that a cow
could jump over the moon
and a dish and a spoon
became sentient beings somehow

MERELY   it was a very tall person that said
'I have caught a cold in my head
and as for heights
they give me the frights
I'm much happier staying in bed'

* * *

48

this is appropriate and should it remain so,
protection for the common man;
there is some dispute as to whether
or not this system does or doesn't work
the problem is illuminated if or when
number counting becomes compulsory

this is considered by many to be
an inappropriate way to achieve
some access to an afterlife

the apple, the apple, the apple
tree for fie sex even – wait!
tell Albert[2] the heretic fails
to appreciate the seriousness without

look up, look down, look around
you can see the avoidable truth
that the old die young and
the middle-aged are in pursuit of
the lost child from a past life

there are no babies in heaven
no cripples, no criminally insane
and there is no democracy
(you don't get to vote)
so very little will have changed

2 Albert Camus

why is there a God? well there isn't
and why oh why oh why
do we question everything from
the here to the now to
the fabric of space-time?
when inherent in the myth of man is
an apparent ability to seek out answers
to that which is blindingly obvious

time moves on and i count my chickens
(one and two and three and four)
but never my eggs until they hatch
(five and six and seven and eight)

time still moves and i still count
(nine and ten and eleven and twelve...)

the number of disciples and
days of Christmas
jurors at a trial
months in a year
inches in a foot...

enough
enough
enough

* * *

49

all pages passed all time and blow
the wind away a laugh and sound
the bells again the hawk below
a shadow cloud upon the ground

the earth it moved is moving still
to space and understanding man
who cannot pray but praise him as
he seeks to find; catch as catch can

water falls and fills the throat
mistaken by some to be a cry
a hand hovers on a more gentle note
and lovers merge with just a sigh

* * *

50

A Poem Of Sorts
For Valerie[3]

In this book, a bible of sorts,
two flowers pressed: one her most treasured
(the first in her garden, the first of spring)
the other, a wild winding wonder (its name escapes me).

In this book, a treasury of sorts,
a poem by a friend I knew not; long dead.
His name escapes me, the sentiment does not.

In this book poems dried and gathered,
the binding worn through use and affection.
It has become a bible of sorts;
truth is contained in more than words.

* * *

3 Valerie Quigley: 6 December 1953 - 18 November 2009

Lightning Source UK Ltd.
Milton Keynes UK
30 June 2010

156347UK00002B/36/P